Solstices

SOLSTICES

by

LOUIS MACNEICE

FABER AND FABER

24 Russell Square

London

First published in mcmlxi
by Faber and Faber Limited
24 Russell Square London WC1
Printed in Great Britain
at the Bowering Press Plymouth

. . . age iam meorum
finis amorum . . .

Contents

Note

Some of these poems have already
appeared in *Encounter, The London Maga-
zine, The New Statesman, The Observer,*
and *Vogue.* Two of them—*The Riddle*
and *Rites of War*—were included in my
Eighty-Five Poems but are reprinted here
because, chronologically, this is where
they belong.

L.M.

Apple Blossom

The first blossom was the best blossom
For the child who never had seen an orchard;
For the youth whom whisky had led astray
The morning after was the first day.

The first apple was the best apple
For Adam before he heard the sentence;
When the flaming sword endorsed the Fall
The trees were his to plant for all.

The first ocean was the best ocean
For the child from streets of doubt and litter;
For the youth for whom the skies unfurled
His first love was his first world.

But the first verdict seemed the worst verdict
When Adam and Eve were expelled from Eden;
Yet when the bitter gates clanged to
The sky beyond was just as blue.

For the next ocean is the first ocean
And the last ocean is the first ocean
And, however often the sun may rise,
A new thing dawns upon our eyes.

For the last blossom is the first blossom
And the first blossom is the best blossom
And when from Eden we take our way
The morning after is the first day.

Invocation

Dolphin plunge, fountain play.
Fetch me far and far away.

Fetch me far my nursery toys,
Fetch me far my mother's hand,
Fetch me far the painted joys.

And when the painted cock shall crow
Fetch me far my waking day
That I may dance before I go.

Fetch me far the breeze in the heat,
Fetch me far the curl of the wave,
Fetch me far the face in the street.

And when the other faces throng
Fetch me far a place in the mind
Where only truthful things belong.

Fetch me far a moon in a tree,
Fetch me far a phrase of the wind,
Fetch me far the verb To Be.

And when the last horn burns the hills
Fetch me far one draught of grace
To quench my thirst before it kills.

Dolphin plunge, fountain play.
Fetch me far and far away.

The Riddle

'What is it that goes round and round the house'
The riddle began. A wolf, we thought, or a ghost?
Our cold backs turned to the chink in the kitchen shutter,
The range made our small scared faces warm as toast.

But now the cook is dead and the cooking, no doubt, electric,
No room for draught or dream, for child or mouse,
Though we, in another place, still put ourselves the question:
What *is* it that goes round and round the house?

Notes for a Biography

I

An oranges (sweet) and lemons (bitter) childhood:
Voices of duty or magic; the first cuckoo;
The longing back and aspiring forward; the double
Feeling that all is new and that all has happened before.

For example, there was a shore
(Oh catnap-happy, catacomb-haunted childhood)
Where head-down first he brooded on pebble and limpet,
Then raised his head to gulp the world entire—

Bumpers of foam and fire,
The horizon carving his guts like a Turkish sword
(Oh gay fire-walking, sad sword-swallowing childhood)
Leaving an ache in his guts and a troubled night.

Call it despair or delight
(Or both), it went. The ringers in St. Clement's
Rang their bells down and under the arch of hands
He escaped, or was carried away, from those ups and downs
    of childhood.

II

Splinters under the nails, weals on the buttocks,
Schooled to service (or was it a pride of class?)
He graduated at length to a land of babus and banyans
And fought their topsyturvy and held the pass
And was just, so he thought; but lonely.

Until the pass was sold (or was it redeemed?)
And he, who had been so homesick, went home reluctant,
Among his own kind a stranger—and one who dreamed
Of a million strangers who fawned or looked askance,
Yet kept his life worth living.

For now, in the heart of his family, under a night
That knew no jackal or tomtom, he would feel
A ghostly net close round him outside which
Were office, children, wife, and the next well-caloried meal,
But inside which was India.

So the small hours filled with bugs and lathi charges
While the questions hammered away: Had it been strength
Or weakness what he had done and what his rulers had done?
After years of this he arrived at a peace of mind to which
He had graduated at length.

III

White rolling battlements on rumbling lead,
A waste of brine which left him thwarted, blinded,
These waves reminded him of love because
All seas are cruel, spendthrift, endless—or was
It that no love remained of which to be reminded?

So other scenes, which once were scenes of longing
Filled with the absence of one person, now
Revert to sheerer emptiness; the thronging
Memories only serve to witness how
Absent has grown the feeling of her absence.

B   [17]

And yet no doubt, ten years or twenty on,
Scars almost lost and the blood grown cooler, kinder,
Things will come back to him that were never gone
And the shifting sea will stand for permanence,
Wave upon wave, reminder upon reminder.

IV

'To the Lords of Convention'—The horses went by
In the racket and dust of the chukker and I
Could assume in my youth that the system was sound
And the world little more than one great polo ground.

But the years they went past and I noticed a change:
The world had grown larger and out of my range.
With the horses gone out and ideas come in,
Where we thought we had ended they bade us begin.

But before we had hardly begun to revise
Those age-old assumptions that clouded our eyes,
What had been in the background now came to the fore
And we found once again that the world was at war.

Then the Lords of Convention they rose up and spoke:
'Your values are senile, your system is broke;
You may still talk of duty but we talk of power,
So open the atlas, for this is the Hour.

Now follow our pointer; look, here is Japan
Where man must now make what he chooses of man,
And these towns are selected to pay for their crime—
A milestone in history, a gravestone in time.'

When I first read the news, to my shame I was glad;
When I next read the news I thought man had gone mad,
And every day since the more news that I read
I too would plead guilty—but where can I plead?

For no one will listen, however I rage;
I am not of their temper and not of this age.
Outnumbered, outmoded, I only can pray
Common sense, if not love, will still carry the day.

V

Lavender blue for love, lavender green for youth—
Never is time to retire.
Let me buy one more bunch and hold myself straight as I can
Not out of pride but out of respect for the truth,
For the gorgeous, though borrowed, fire
Which shone on my cradle and warmed my heart as a man.

Street-cries under my window. Who will buy?
Never is time to retire.
Age and arthritis have crippled me, even so
I will respond to the blue and green in the cry
And purchase all I desire
For just a few pennies or annas, one gesture before I go.

Lavender green for youth, lavender blue for love—
Never is time to retire.
I have had both and unstinted and now, whatever
Doubt may rise from below or terror brood from above,
I will stand as if under fire
With a sweet-smelling bunch in my hand, face to face with
    Never.

The Slow Starter

A watched clock never moves, they said:
Leave it alone and you'll grow up.
Nor will the sulking holiday train
Start sooner if you stamp your feet.
　　He left the clock to go its way;
　　The whistle blew, the train went gay.

Do not press me so, she said;
Leave me alone and I will write
But not just yet, I am sure you know
The problem. Do not count the days.
　　He left the calendar alone;
　　The postman knocked, no letter came.

O never force the pace, they said;
Leave it alone, you have lots of time,
Your kind of work is none the worse
For slow maturing. Do not rush.
　　He took their tip, he took his time,
　　And found his time and talent gone.

Oh you have had your chance, It said;
Left it alone and it was one.
Who said a watched clock never moves?
Look at it now. Your chance was I.
　　He turned and saw the accusing clock
　　Race like a torrent round a rock.

Il Piccolo Rifiuto

Impatient with cripples, foreigners, children,
As though they were midges or wasps he refused
Jam on his bread or to walk in the shrubbery.
Crutch and giggle and guttural accent
Were left in the air. He was disabused
Of a world not his, his birth certificate
Faded behind his eyes, his eyes
Blinked as the jets dived on the jampot
He had not ordered and harpy-wise
The insect world grew breasts and talons
And wogs and wops kept babbling and mad
Children went on a spacelark and God
Began to limp and deep in the bad
Shrubbery shrubs that should be ever
Green turned brown. He asked for a stone
But the waiter offered him bread in yiddish.
No, he repeated, I never ordered
Jam, God damn you, leave me alone.

The Messiah

(a memory of 1940)

In Portsmouth, New Hampshire, plugged with morphia,
Cranked up on my hospital bed to see through the window,
I watched in a building one hundred yards away
A light flashing on and off in a window,
Half an hour maybe between the flashes,
And I split in two, one naïve, one know-all:
What's going on over there?

                    Why, don't you know, they are smelting.
(Pause). But who is?

                    The great new surgeon of course.
(Pause). New Surgeon?

                    Greatest surgeon in the world;
A completely new technique. How odd that you haven't
   heard of him.
I'm afraid I've not.

                    But he's also the new Messiah.
(Longer pause). The what?

                    A new mutation of man,
He knows the answers to everything.

                    Everything?

                    Yes, except
He cannot cure himself. It's very sad, you know.
(Pause). What is so sad?

                    He's a refugee from Europe.
(Pause). But so are many.

                    Of course, but he is sadder;
He's lost his name, you know.

                    (Pause). He's lost his name?
Yes, whenever one has to introduce him,

To prove who he is, you see, or that he is,
All he can do is hiccup. See where that light is flashing—
Just be quiet and listen and you may hear him hiccup.
I listened and did and began to hiccup too
And the night nurse came in and gave me another shot.
The building that flashed the light was the Maternity Ward.

The Atlantic Tunnel

(a memory of 1940)

America was ablaze with lights,
Eastward the sea was black, the ship
Black, not a cigarette on deck;
It was like entering a zigzag tunnel.

Old Irish nuns were returning home,
So were young men due for the call-up,
So were the survivors from the Jervis Bay;
The tunnel absorbed us, made us one.

But how many miles or days we did not
Know we were one, nor how many waves
Carried in code the words to prevent,
The words to destroy. We were just passengers,

As on this ship, so on our own
Lives, passengers, parasites, never
Entrusted with headphones or signals and out of
The code, yet not in the clear. The tunnel

Might be about to collapse, this whole
Zigzag might be a widening crack
Which led to the bottom before Belfast
Or Liverpool gave us reluctant welcome.

Meanwhile the dark ship rolled, a ball
Prattled and spun on a rolling table;
The sailors from the Jervis Bay
Called the score, were otherwise silent.

Homage to Wren

(a memory of 1941)

At sea in the dome of St Paul's
Riding the firefull night,
Fountains of sparks like a funfair,
We patrolled between the inner and outer walls,
Saw that all hatches were screwed down tight
And felt that Sir Christopher Wren had made everything
   shipshape.

Then went on deck with the spray
Of bombs in our ears and watched
The fire clouds caught in our rigging, the gaudy signals:
London Expects—but the rest of the string was vague,
Ambiguous rather and London was rolling away
Three hundred years to the aftermath of the plague,

And the flames were whippeting, dolphining, over the streets,
The red whale spouting out of submerged Londinium
And Davy Jones's locker burst wide open
To throw to the surface ledgers and lavatory seats
And all the bric-a-brac of warehouses and churches
With bones and ghosts and half forgotten quotations.

Then the storm subsided and it was dawn, it was cold,
I climbed to the crow's nest for one last look at the roaring
   foam,
League upon league of scarlet and gold,
But it was cold so I stretched out my hands from the drunken
   mast
And warmed my hands at London and went home.

Rites of War

So, Fortinbras; Alas is now the keyword here.
A waste you say? Yet graced with swagged and canopied
    verse,
All tragedies of kings having wings to raise their gloom
(Even as the lights go down the crowns come up) but you,
    sir,
Have seen far more of gore without this pomp, have heard
Your dying soldiers cry though not in iambics, not
In any manner of speech to reach the future's ear,
Their death being merely breath that ceased and flesh that
    slumped
As both, it is true, must do ten years, ten centuries, hence,
On a cutprice night, not a flight of angels near to sing
Their souls to whatever rest were best if souls they had.
Still, at this stage and age before, if ever, we read
The story, the glory, in full of your Polack wars and the long
List of your dead—you said a waste, did you not?—we also
Trust for the future's sake you will take your immediate cue,
That curtain, that certain line—and the last chance to boot
For Fortinbras to pass. Go, bid the soldiers shoot.

Jericho

Oh the sun stood still above the Passport Office
And Joshua remembered Moses.
They chewed gum, they sweated gore,
Their visas were refused once more
And the Tables of the Law were broken again.

And the sun stood still above the Law Courts in Fleet Street
And Joshua remembered Moses.
Adulteries and libels both
Got bogged in medieval sloth
And the Tables of the Law were broken again.

And the sun stood still above the hard courts in Hampstead
And Joshua remembered Moses.
Refugees from worlds away
Worked out their loneliness in play
And the Tables of the Law were broken again.

And the sun stood still above the Stock Exchange
And Joshua remembered Moses.
Thousands of ants in pinstriped pants
Went back upon their tracks like ants
And the Tables of the Law were broken again.

And the sun stood still above the dome of Paul's
And Joshua remembered Moses.
The fires were out from the war we lost,
Also the fires of Pentecost,
And the Tables of the Law were broken again.

And the sun stood still above Notting Hill Gate
And Joshua remembered Moses.
The Caribbean in spite of cosh
And flick-knife wouldn't come out in the wash
And the Tables of the Law were broken again.

And the sun stood still above the Ministry of Defence
And Joshua remembered Moses.
Neither sense nor conscience stirred,
Having been ultimately deterred,
And the Tables of the Law were broken again.

Yours Next

Fruit machines and pin tables—
Someone has got to pay for the round.
Only release the spring, the ball
Will scurry, the coins will clatter and all
That was ill lost may well be found.

Contract and lease and marriage lines—
Someone has got to pay for the round.
Only sign on the line and all
The gains you doubt may come on call
And rate one farthing in the pound.

Stake and faggot and gas chamber—
Someone has got to pay for the round.
Only press the button and all
The springs will twang, the heads will fall,
And yet, whatever drinks are downed,
Someone has got to pay for the round.

Dark Age Glosses

on the Venerable Bede

Birds flitting in and out of the barn
Bring back an Anglo-Saxon story:
The great wooden hall with long fires down the centre,
Their feet in the rushes, their hands tearing the meat.
Suddenly high above them they notice a swallow enter
From the black storm and zigzag over their heads,
Then out once more into the unknown night;
And that, someone remarks, is the life of man.
But now it is time to sleep; one by one
They rise from the bench and their gigantic shadows
Lurch on the shuddering walls. How can the world
Or the non-world beyond harbour a bird?
They close their eyes that smart from the woodsmoke: how
Can anyone even guess his whence and whither?
This indoors flying makes it seem absurd,
Although it itches and nags and flutters and yearns,
To postulate any other life than now.

on the Grettir Saga

The burly major they denied
The Victoria Cross because of his drinking habits,
Blown up soon after, for some reason reminds me
Of the strong man of Iceland who also died
Under the frown of the safe men, cooped in an islet
With a festering leg and a bad record:
An outrageous outlaw, his mind ill equipped,
His temper uncertain, too quick with his weapons,
Yet had done the scattered farms some service,

Also had made people laugh, like the major
Raising his elbow in the mess at 'Pindi;
But, unlike the major, Grettir was cursed,
Haunted by eyes in the dark, on his desolate
Rock on the fringe of the Arctic knew
The fear no man had ever induced in him,
And thus awaited his doom. Whereas
The major, who also was doomed, slept sound
And was merely cursed by the curse of his time.

on the Njal Saga

The tall blonde dabbing scent behind her ears
And throwing over her shoulder her Parthian curse
To leave her lover facing the world defenceless
Calls up the picture through one thousand years
Of a tall blonde with her hair to her waist, exulting
Over her husband with his bow-string cut
Because he had begged one strand of her hair to mend it.
'Yes indeed, my hair could save your life now—But
Do you remember that slap you gave me once?'
So Gunnar stood with the roof off over his head
And his enemies closed in. She watched and smiled.
Almost reluctantly they left him dead
And they and she thus left a legacy
Of many deaths to come—man, woman and child—
And one great saga casting from those dark
Ages a lighthouse ray, a reminder that even then,
For all the spite and hatred and betrayal,
Men had the nobler qualities of men.

The light was no doubt the same, the ecology different:
All Ireland drowned in woods. Those who today
Think it a golden age and at Glendalough
Or Clonmacnois let imagination play
Like flame upon those ruins should keep in mind
That the original actual flames were often
Kindled not by the Norsemen but by the monks'
Compatriots, boorish kings who, mad to find
Loot to outride each other's ambition, would stop
At nothing—which so often led to nothing.
Which is even—tell it not in the Gaelic League—
True of the High King Brian whose eighty years,
Caught in a web of largely his own intrigue,
Soured him with power and rusted him with blood
To let him die in a tent on a cold Good Friday
To earn his niche. And yet he earned his niche.
The last battle was his; maybe the sun came out
Before the defeated Norseman struck him, before
History endorsed the triumph and the rout.
The light was no doubt the same—and just as rich.

Indoor Sports

Darts

Begin and end with a double. He places his feet
Square apart on the rubber mat. I bet I shall end
As always on double one. The squeaking chalk
Subtracts, subtracts. . . . What did I tell you? And why
Is it the hardest bed? Singles are useless
And there is no going back.
                       He flicks his wrist,
Hardly looking, and wins.

Shove Halfpenny

On the field of elm or slate the lines are far too close;
The brass discs knock each other out of place.
You need a glancing blow with the ball of the thumb;
One disc can knock another one into place
With skill and join her there. No, not like that;
Like this.
            You see. Both safely between the lines.
With skill, as I said. And luck.

Vingt-et-Un

Stay, twist, or buy. Ace is eleven or one.
Not really much scope for skill, I could play this game in
    my sleep;
Still, talking of sleep, it too can pass the time.
Yes, what do you think? I'm going for five and under;
I ought to twist but I'll buy.
                   The small cards fall;
I'm buying again, I ought to be bust, but there—
It paid me not to twist!

c

Ninety-nine down: a one letter word meaning something
    indefinite.
The indefinite article or—would it perhaps be the personal
    pronoun?
But what runs across it? Four letter word meaning something
With a bias towards its opposite, the second letter
Must be the same as the one letter word.

                                    It is time
We left these puzzles and started to be ourselves
And started to live, is it not?

Idle Talk

Flightily falling words like yellow
Leaves are blown into coigns of memory;
The little trees of our youth are bare
While on tall steel masts the big words bloom

To put in the shade, and to shame, our idle
Gossip, to fill our skies with a smell
Like an open drain: ratchet and fang,
Weirds of our children, man-eating flowers.

And yet we continue, frivolous, garrulous,
Plotting our chatter, planting our annuals—
Anecdote, limerick, tittle-tattle, chestnut—
But, come full circle, the leaves are green.

And, come full circle, the chestnut candles
Abide the spark of tapered wit,
While the rotten compost of hackneyed phrase
Reprieves the captive, feeds the future.

For, whether to find oneself or find
Those other selves through whom one lives,
The little words that get in the way
Can also pave the way for a wish.

Shop-talk, club-talk, cliché, slang—
The wind that makes the dead leaf fall
Can also make the live leaf dance,
Though the green of this was the green of that

And all our gems have been worn before
And what we intend as new was never
Not used by someone centuries back
Or by oneself some weeks before.

In despite of which, though the First Garden
Is supposed to be closed to all for ever,
The innocence that our days outmode
Seems no more innocent than that

Adam achieved when, holding the half-
bitten, already half-forgotten,
Fruit in his hand, he looked at Eve
And, wholly forgetting Eve herself

As he had known her till that moment,
Looked and felt for the same three words
Which he had uttered time and again
But never like this, and said: 'I love you'.

Country Week-End

I

Coffee leaps in a crystal knob,
Chugs and glints while birds gossip;
We have been here a thousand years
Nor yet have reached the age of gas.

And a thousand years of songbirds' bones
Are pasted in these cottage walls,
While a thousand years of harvest mice
Wait for our cat to pounce the next.

Outgoing heirlooms: cups and plates,
Nettle and colt's foot, elder hedge,
Blackthorn beyond, then field on field,
And then the skyline; then the sky.

Not ready yet? It takes its cue,
Boils over, and the rats in the thatch
Boil over too, while children's laughter
Rattles the plates and scares the birds,

As once it did when plates were wood,
Coffee unknown and fields unhedged,
Though then as now the sky was ours
Of which our souls were part and parcel,

Tied with blue ribbon or coarse twine.
But rat and bird are settling back
As, eggspoon poised, the youngest child
Assumes this day his lasting life.

Not ready yet? For what may spill
Or shine or pipe or pounce? This world,
Ingrown, outgoing, soon outgone,
Stays ours. We are ready now as then.

II

Forth from a sack of fishing-reels and deck-quoits
Emerge the stubborn boots which once,
Part of my Home Guard outfit, hammered sparks
From Regent Street but are rusticated now

To aid yet another makebelieve, to seal
The countryside with hobnails, while my walk
Becomes a countryman's. As if discomfort
Around the feet could loose and lift the mind.

Boots also link us with the world of folk-tales:
What third son setting forth to bilk an ogre
Or pluck a bride from her redoubt of thorn
Ever wore shoes? I also need my beanstalk—

Hand me that dibble. That the earth is good
Stands trial this week-end. Let it get under
My finger-nails, add weight to what I have read
And wish to think I feel; and to my boots.

Even blisters help, which these same plodhoofs gave me
In the Constable country on an Easter Monday;
It was Nineteen Forty-Four and the day was full
Of cowslips, birds and beer, but the night, we knew,

[38]

Would be full of southbound bombers and a moon
Of which one old farm-labourer raising his eyes
From a pint that might have been a ball of crystal
Said: 'You know, we call this Monty's Moon.'

III

Wild grass in spate in a rainy wind,
We have come from London to stay indoors
With paraffin on our hands, our eyes
Watching through glass the trees blown east.

As if hypnotised, as if this wet
Day were the sum and essence of days
When such spinning shafts of steely water
Struck to numb, or revive, the mind.

As once in a low-slung floating island,
Hardly afloat that day, Tiree,
We stopped indoors in the small hotel
And a young Glaswegian in broad checks

Told our fortunes while sniggering faces
Froze in surprise and fear as the cards
Kept turning up and the rain kept falling.
Or as once, in an Irish island, the turf

Hissed in the fire and I felt marooned
In a whitewashed room in a world of water
Part rain, part brine, where one small ark
Was casting off to find Atlantis,

But I did not dare embark. Or as often,
Much further back, a child I pressed
My nose against the streaming pane
That framed the road to the neighbouring graveyard

On which with luck could be seen beneath
The sodden trees the huddled mourners
At a slow squelch behind the box
Crossing the pane, through the rain darkly.

And so today as these different windows
Blotch and weep in Southern England
Our defences, both of stone and skin,
Seem weak to hold this peace inside

Four walls—Worth what compared with that
First element, those fluent spears?
Spearmen or not, ourselves, in dreams,
This element, once ours, though lost,

In dreams may still be fought and wooed;
So let this rain keep falling, let
This wind from the west be backed by waves
On which the mind can embark anew.

IV

Here too, as in my childhood, twilight
Means pouring in and turning up,
Striking a match, lighting a wick,
A ritual for the hands, a pause

Between the light which, we were always
Told, was not good enough to read by,
And this new light which needed watching
And which, whether good enough or not,

Made print and content both seem different.
So now these oil lamps make a different
Evening from our usual, span
A gap of decades, calling back

Bustling dead women with steady hands,
One from Tyrone and one from Cavan
And one my mother; the soft lights marched
Nightly out of the pantry and spread

Assurance, not like the fickle candles
Which gave the dark a jagged edge
And made it darker yet, more evil,
Whereas these lamps, we knew, were kind

Like good Penates, from their globes
Or tasselled tents conferring peace
Even on the Lays of Ancient Rome.
Just so my reading of middle age

Reads better in this light, without
The chance of a failure at the main
Or a short, without—what matters more—
That sameness governed by a switch

Which could epitomise our times
Where everything, not only light
But food and freedom, thought and life,
Can be switched on just so—or off.

So now it is time. Decant the oil,
Turn up the wick. Call it escape
Or what rude name you like—or call it
A good deed, rather a good night:
One good night in a naughty world.

Nature Notes

Dandelions

Incorrigible, brash,
They brightened the cinder path of my childhood,
Unsubtle, the opposite of primroses,
But, unlike primroses, capable
Of growing anywhere, railway track, pierhead,
Like our extrovert friends who never
Make us fall in love, yet fill
The primroseless roseless gaps.

Cats

Incorrigible, uncommitted,
They leavened the long flat hours of my childhood,
Subtle, the opposite of dogs,
And, unlike dogs, capable
Of flirting, falling, and yawning anywhere,
Like women who want no contract
But going their own way
Make the way of their lovers lighter.

Corncrakes

Incorrigible, unmusical,
They bridged the surrounding hedge of my childhood,
Unsubtle, the opposite of blackbirds,
But, unlike blackbirds, capable
Anywhere they are of endorsing summer
Like loud men around the corner
Whom we never see but whose raucous
Voices can give us confidence.

The Sea

Incorrigible, ruthless,
It rattled the shingly beach of my childhood,
Subtle, the opposite of earth,
And, unlike earth, capable
Any time at all of proclaiming eternity
Like something or someone to whom
We have to surrender, finding
Through that surrender life.

Sleeping Winds

North

The wind was curled in a ball asleep in a tree
With a young man cutting a heart on the bark;
Something came into the absence of mind of the wind,
He threw off the green and yawned himself over the sky;
The young man also grew to the height of a cloud
And was loud and rapid and free and never to die.

East

The wind was slumped on a charpoy in the bazaar,
Her breasts heavy with history; something crept
Slily under her sari at dead of noon
And while the city slept she craved for water
And jumped to her feet and brushed the flies from her eyes
And took her pitcher and ran to the well of her own
    monsoon.

West

The wind lay still on the deck of Brandan's ship
While the sailors tried to rouse her; she never stirred
Till Brandan joined his hands and, coincidence or not,
She got on her knees and filled her lungs and put
Her lips to the sail and puffed. The long lost ship
Flew home and into legend like a bird.

South

The wind had hidden his head in a pit in the sand
Of an uncrossable desert; something slid

Into his lack of ear, he gradually uncurled
Like a king cobra, rose and spread his hood
And swayed in time with what the charmer piped,
In time with Time, to wreck or bless the world.

The Park

Through a glass greenly men as trees walking
Led by their dogs, trees as torrents
Loosed by the thaw, tulips as shriekmarks
(Yelps of delight), lovers as coracles
Riding the rapids: Spring as a spring
Releasing the jack-in-a-box of a fanfare.

Urban enclave of lawns and water,
Lacquered ducks and young men sculling,
Children who never had seen the country
Believing it this while those who had once
Known real country ignore the void
Their present imposes, their past exposes.

South and east lie the yellowed terraces
Grandiose, jerrybuilt, ghosts of gracious
Living, and north those different terraces
Where great white bears with extensile necks,
Convicted sentries, lope their beat,
No rest for their paws till the day they die.

Fossils of flesh, fossils of stucco:
Between them the carefully labelled flower beds
And the litter baskets, but also between them
Through a grill gaily men as music
Forcing the spring to loose the lid,
To break the bars, to find the world.

The Lake in the Park

On an empty morning a small clerk
Who thinks no one will ever love him
Sculls on the lake in the park while bosomy
Trees indifferently droop above him.

On the bank a father and mother goose
Hiss as he passes, pigeons are courting,
Everything mocks; the empty deck-chairs
Are set in pairs, there is no consorting

For him with nature or man, the ducks
Go arrowheading across his bows
Adding insult to absence, his mood
Disallows what the sun endows.

The water arrows are barbed; their barbs,
Corrugated like flint, can start
No Stone Age echoes in his mind
And yet they too might pierce his heart.

Dogs in the Park

The precise yet furtive etiquette of dogs
Makes them ignore the whistle while they talk
In circles round each other, one-man bonds
Deferred in pauses of this man-made walk
To open vistas to a past of packs

That raven round the stuccoed terraces
And scavenge at the mouth of Stone Age caves;
What man proposes dog on his day disposes
In litter round both human and canine graves,
Then lifts his leg to wash the gravestones clean,

While simultaneously his eyes express
Apology and contempt; his master calls
And at the last and sidelong he returns,
Part heretic, part hack, and jumps and crawls
And fumbles to communicate and fails.

And then they leave the park, the leads are snapped
On to the spiky collars, the tails wag
For no known reason and the ears are pricked
To search through legendary copse and crag
For legendary creatures doomed to die
Even as they, the dogs, were doomed to live.

Sunday in the Park

No sunlight ever. Bleak trees whisper ironies,
Carolina duck and Canada goose forget
Their world across the water, red geraniums
Enhance the chill, dark glasses mirror ironies,
The prams are big with doom, the walkers-out forget
Why they are out, London is lost, geraniums
Stick it out in the wind, old men feel lost
But stick it out and refugees forget
Pretences and grow sad while ironies
Frill out from sprinklers on the green veneer
That screens the tubes in which congested trains
Get stuck like enemas or ironies
Half lost between the lines while dachshunds run
Like centipedes and no one knows the time
Whatever foreigners ask it. Here is Sunday:
And on the seventh day He rested. The Tree
Forgets both good and evil in irony.

Windowscape

Green skeletons of fish, they swim across the pale
Blue wind, acacia leaves. The summer is turning stale,
The panes are dusty, the birds are silent, this whole
Suburb is lost in the dream of one lost soul
Who looking outward marks a road where no one lives
And feeling backward craves a gift that no one gives.
This is Number One The Grove, the shops are far and dear,
Window-cleaner and postman call just once a year
And never a priest. Looking up and out from his room he sees
An aerial on a roof, a pattern of crossed keys,
Crossed bones that are failed fingers. He pauses never to
    think;
The pause is one long trance of an eye that cannot blink,
The eyelids being sewn up; the pause is a failed flow
Of a mind that does not even know that it does not know.
Thus he looks up and whether he has been fed
Or not he does not know, feels neither alive nor dead,
Has neither diary nor menu, form nor fate,
Nor can look down to see what is left on the plate.
So many fingers to cross, so many windows to clean,
So many summers to bone. And yet those bones are green.

Solstice

How did midsummer come so soon,
The lean trees racing into lush?
He had turned his back one moment, then turned
And took it full in the face—the gush
Of green, the stare of blue, the sieve
Of sun and shadow, the wish to live.

And what was nowhere now was here
And here was all and all was good;
Between the lines the words were strange
Yet not to be misunderstood.
The glad flowers talked with tongues of flame
And who was he was not the same.

Nor was there question who was she
For whom his years were blessed to wait,
Whose opening eyes to him were now,
As his to hers, an open gate,
One entrance to one constant song.
How can midsummer stay so long?

Indian Village

Whatever it is that jigs and gleams—
Flickering lizard, courting bird—
For which I could not, had I even
One hour to implement my dreams,
Concoct one new and apposite word,
Might yet prove heaven this side heaven,

Viz. life. Euripides was right
To say 'whatever glints' (or dances),
Thus answering those who mark the spot
Meticulously in black and white
And who, contemptuous of the chances,
Divorce the ever from the what.

So here, beneath this pepperpot temple,
Black buffalo eyedeep in the pond,
The sunset purples walls of mud
While hard and gnarled grow smooth and simple
And hunkered peasants gaze beyond
Their hookahs at that orb of blood

Which founders towards its rising day,
A one-eyed starer with a knife,
A ranter flushed with fire and wine;
When we shall also rise and say
A small piece but our own, and life,
Whatever it is, must leap and shine.

Jungle Clearance Ceylon

In a manmade lake at first light
Cruising between the tops of bleached
Skeleton trees we waited for elephant
Coming to drink. They never came
But, focussing in, on each bare branch
Of the bonewhite trees we marked a pelican
Frozen to fossil, looking down
Its beak in contempt of human beings
Who had drowned a valley to found a town—
Power and water for human beings
In the thick of the bush. In the thin of the trees
The pelican perched as though in a glass
Case where the wind could never blow
Nor elephant come to drink nor human
Beings presume in the grey dawn
To press a button or throw a switch
To slap the west on the back of the east
In spite of archaic and absent elephant
In spite of archaic and present pelican
In spite of themselves as human beings.

Half Truth from Cape Town

Between a smoking fire and a tolling bell
When I was young and at home I could not tell
What problems roosting ten miles to the west
Waited like vultures in their gantried nest
Till Prod should tumble Papish in the river.
I could not tell. The bell went on for ever.

Now through the swinging doors of the decades I
Confront a waste of tarmac, a roaring sky;
The Southern Cross supplants the Useful Plough—
But where are Livingstone and his Lion now?
That cross was raised to mark this safe hotel
Between the goldmines and the padded cell.

In each glib airport between here and you
As the loudspeaker speaks the ants pour through,
Some going north into their past and some
South to this future that may never come,
But all engrossed to that same point that good
Ants would die to get to if they could.

So here I rest, with Devil's Peak above,
Between a smoking fire and a calling dove,
Its voice like a crazy clock that every ten
Minutes runs down, so must be wound again;
And who is all but come or all but gone
I cannot tell. The dove goes on, goes on.

Solitary Travel

Breakfasting alone in Karachi, Delhi, Calcutta,
Dacca, Singapore, Kuala Lumpur, Colombo, Cape Town,
But always under water or glass, I find
Such a beginning makes the day seem blind.

The hotels are all the same, it might be pawpaw
Instead of grapefruit, different flowers on the table,
But the waiters, coffee-coloured or yellow or black,
All smile but, should you smile, give nothing back.

And taking coffee alone in the indistinguishable airports,
Though the land outside be empty or man-crammed, oven
    or icebox,
I feel the futility of moving on
To what, though not a conclusion, stays foregone.

But the Customs clamour, the stamp is raised, the passport
Like a chess game played by mail records the latest
Move of just one square. Which is surely seen
By the black bishop and the unsleeping queen.

And so to the next hotel to the selfsame breakfast,
Same faces of manager, waiter, fellow-traveller,
Same lounge or bar whose test tube walls enfold
The self-indulgent disenchanted old.

Time and the will lie sidestepped. If I could only
Escape into icebox or oven, escape among people
Before tomorrow from this neutral zone
Where all tomorrows must be faced alone. . . .

Old Masters Abroad

Painfully grinning faces like dogs' or
Inattentive like cats' all over
The static globe affect to be lectured
By the singing birds of unknown England.

Shakespeare flaunts his codpiece at dhoti,
Ditto at sari, Pope with his clouded
Cane conducts the dancers of Bali,
The lesser celandine sprouts in Lagos.

And the skylark crying 'Bird I never!'
Routs parrakeet, hornbill, kookaburra,
While the nightingale puts on spurs in Hampstead
To rip the guts from the decadent bulbul.

Wee sleekit courin' timorous warthog!
Tirra lirra by Kabul River!
The elmtree bole is in tiny leaf but
Not for long because of the termites.

At Bablockhythe the stripling Ganges
Burns on her ghats the scholar gypsy,
There's a deathly hush on the rocks of Aden,
Nine bean rows rise in the Kalahari.

The faces listen or not. The lecturers
Mop their memories. All over the static
Globe the needle sticks in the groove.
It is overtime now for the Old Masters.

Icebergs

If icebergs were warm below the water
One would not wince at their jagged tops;
Lifting and dipping on the swell
They still might signal all was well.

But icebergs are cold in the dark water,
Cold their base as white their crest,
And those who dive to check the fact
Can find no signal to retract.

There are no words below the water,
Let alone phrases, let alone
Sentences—except the one
Sentence that tells you life is done

And what you had of it was a mere
Ninth or tenth; the rest is sheer
Snub to those who dared suppose
Icebergs warm below the water.

Vistas

Emerging from aeons of ocean on to the shore
The creature found itself in a roadless
Forest where nothing stretched before
Its lack of limbs but lack of hope
Until the trees, millennia later,
Parted to grant it greater scope.

Emerging from miles of tunnel into a plain
The train finds itself in a foreign
Beatitude. Creeping fog and rain
And deafmute fears are left behind;
The stuttering grub grows wings and sings
The tune it never thought to find.

Emerging from years of lacking into a love
The Self finds itself in predestined
Freedom. Around, below, above,
Glinting fish and piping birds
Deny that earth and truth are only
Earth, respectively, and words.

Variation on Heraclitus

Even the walls are flowing, even the ceiling,
Nor only in terms of physics; the pictures
Bob on each picture rail like floats on a line
While the books on the shelves keep reeling
Their titles out into space and the carpet
Keeps flying away to Arabia nor can this be where I stood—
Where I shot the rapids I mean—when I signed
On a line that rippled away with a pen that melted
Nor can this now be the chair—the chairoplane of a chair—
That I sat in the day that I thought I had made up my mind
And as for that standard lamp it too keeps waltzing away
Down an unbridgeable Ganges where nothing is standard
And lights are but lit to be drowned in honour and spite of
    some dark
And vanishing goddess. No, whatever you say,
Reappearance presumes disappearance, it may not be nice
Or proper or easily analysed not to be static
But none of your slide snide rules can catch what is sliding
    so fast
And, all you advisers on this by the time it is that,
I just do not want your advice
Nor need you be troubled to pin me down in my room
Since the room and I will escape for I tell you flat:
One cannot live in the same room twice.

Reflections

The mirror above my fireplace reflects the reflected
Room in my window; I look in the mirror at night
And see two rooms, the first where left is right
And the second, beyond the reflected window, corrected
But there I am standing back to my back. The standard
Lamp comes thrice in my mirror, twice in my window,
The fire in the mirror lies two rooms away through the
    window,
The fire in the window lies one room away down the terrace,
My actual room stands sandwiched between confections
Of night and lights and glass and in both directions
I can see beyond and through the reflections the street lamps
At home outdoors where my indoors rooms lie stranded,
Where a taxi perhaps will drive in through the bookcase
Whose books are not for reading and past the fire
Which gives no warmth and pull up by my desk
At which I cannot write since I am not lefthanded.

Hold-Up

The lights were red, refused to change,
Ash-ends grew longer, no one spoke,
The papers faded in their hands,
The bubbles in the football pools
Went flat, the hot news froze, the dates
They could not keep were dropped like charred
Matches, the girls no longer flagged
Their sex, besides the code was lost,
The engine stalled, a tall glass box
On the pavement held a corpse in pickle
His ear still cocked, and no one spoke,
No number rang, for miles behind
The other buses nudged and blared
And no one dared get out. The conductress
Was dark and lost, refused to change.

Restaurant Car

Fondling only to throttle the nuzzling moment
Smuggled under the table, hungry or not
We roughride over the sleepers, finger the menu,
Avoid our neighbours' eyes and wonder what

Mad country moves beyond the steamed-up window
So fast into the past we could not keep
Our feet on it one instant. Soup or grapefruit?
We had better eat to pass the time, then sleep

To pass the time. The water in the carafe
Shakes its hips, both glass and soup plate spill,
The tomtom beats in the skull, the waiters totter
Along their invisible tightrope. For good or ill,

For fish or meat, with single tickets only,
Our journey still in the nature of a surprise,
Could we, before we stop where all must change,
Take one first risk and catch our neighbours' eyes?

The Wiper

Through purblind night the wiper
Reaps a swathe of water
On the screen; we shudder on
  And hardly hold the road,
All we can see a segment
Of blackly shining asphalt
With the wiper moving across it
  Clearing, blurring, clearing.

But what to say of the road?
The monotony of its hardly
Visible cambe , the mystery
  Of its far invisible margins,
Will these be always with us,
The night being broken only
By lights that pass or meet us
  From others in moving boxes?

Boxes of glass and water,
Upholstered, equipped with dials
Professing to tell the distance
  We have gone, the speed we are going,
But never a gauge nor needle
To tell us where we are going
Or when day will come, supposing
  This road exists in daytime.

For now we cannot remember
Where we were when it was not
Night, when it was not raining,
  Before this car moved forward

[64]

And the wiper backward and forward
Lighting so little before us
Of a road that, crouching forward,
    We watch move always towards us,

Which through the tiny segment
Cleared and blurred by the wiper
Is sucked in under the axle
    To be spewed behind us and lost
While we, dazzled by darkness,
Haul the black future towards us
Peeling the skin from our hands;
    And yet we hold the road.

The Wall

Face to the wall and behind him
The room full of well-wishers.
But what, they said, can we do?
He has abdicated, his life is behind him.

The bed had known birth and death;
Where was the wall had once been a window.
Now all the light is behind him.
The wall is a blind end.

No, they said, no doctor.
Nor priest. What is the use?
There is not even a window
For body or soul to look through.

But, as they spoke, their voices
Faded away while the wall
Grew nearer so that he heard
Different voices beyond it,

Singing. And there was light
Before him as through a window
That opens on to a garden.
The first garden. The last.

The Snow Man

His memory was shaped by forgetting
Into a snowman, handful by handful;
In the end two pebbles for eyes and a cherrywood
Pipe clamped in the thinlipped mouth.

But was this fellow really his past,
This white dummy in a white waste?
While the censor works, while the frost holds,
Perhaps he will pass—but then he will pass.

Yesterday was a dance of flakes
Waltzing down, around, and up,
But today is lull and smudge, today
Is a man with a pipe that will not draw.

Today is a legless day with head-on
Idiot eyes, a stranded deaf
Mute in a muted world. This lump
Is what he remembered when he forgot,

Already beginning to dribble. Tomorrow
Comes the complete forgetting, the thaw.
Or is it rather a dance of water
To replace, relive, that dance of white?

The Truisms

His father gave him a box of truisms
Shaped like a coffin, then his father died;
The truisms remained on the mantelpiece
As wooden as the playbox they had been packed in
Or that other his father skulked inside.

Then he left home, left the truisms behind him
Still on the mantelpiece, met love, met war,
Sordor, disappointment, defeat, betrayal,
Till through disbeliefs he arrived at a house
He could not remember seeing before.

And he walked straight in; it was where he had come
    from
And something told him the way to behave.
He raised his hand and blessed his home;
The truisms flew and perched on his shoulders
And a tall tree sprouted from his father's grave.

The Blasphemies

The sin against the Holy . . . though what
He wondered was it? Cold in his bed
He thought: If I think those words I know
Yet must not be thinking—Come to the hurdle
And I shall be damned through thinking Damn—
But Whom? But no! Those words are unthinkable;
Damn anyone else, but once I—No,
Here lies the unforgivable blasphemy.
So pulling the cold sheets over his head
He swore to himself he had not thought
Those words he knew but never admitted.
To be damned at seven years old was early.

Ten years later, his Who's Who
No longer cosmic, he turned to parody—
Prayers, hymns, the Apostles' Creed—
Preening himself as a gay blasphemer,
But what is a practical joke in a world
Of nonsense, what is a rational attitude
Towards politics in a world of cyphers,
Towards sex if you lack all lust, towards art
If you do not believe in communication?
And what is a joke about God if you do not
Accept His existence? Where is the blasphemy?
No Hell at seventeen feels empty.

Rising thirty, he had decided
God was a mere expletive, a cheap one,
No longer worth a laugh, no longer

A proper occasion to prove one's freedom
By denying something not worth denying.
So humanism was all and the only
Sin was the sin against the Human—
But you could not call it Ghost for that
Was merely emotive; the only—you could not
Call it sin for that was emotive—
The only failure was not to face
The facts. But at thirty what are the facts?

Ten years later, in need of myth,
He thought: I can use my childhood symbols
Divorced from their context, Manger and Cross
Could do very well for Tom Dick and Harry—
Have we not all of us been in a war
So have we not carried call it a cross
Which was never our fault? Yet how can a cross
Be never your fault? The words of the myth,
Now merely that and no longer faith,
Melt in his hands which were never proved
Hard as nails, nor can he longer
Speak for the world—or himself—at forty.

Forty to fifty. In ten years
He grew to feel the issue irrelevant:
Tom Dick and Harry were not Christ
And whether Christ were God or not
And whether there were a God or not
The word was inadequate. For himself
He was not Tom or Dick or Harry,
Let alone God, he was merely fifty,

No one and nowhere else, a walking
Question but no more cheap than any
Question or quest is cheap. The sin
Against the Holy Ghost—What is it?

Bad Dream

The window was made of ice with bears lumbering across it,
      Bears the size of flies;
The ceiling was one great web with flies cantankering in it,
      Flies the size of men;
The floor was riddled with holes with men phutscuttering
down them
      Into the jaws of mice.

Outside there were no other houses, only bedizened
hoardings
      With panties prancing on them
And an endless file of chromium-plated lamp posts
      With corpses dangling from them
And one gaunt ruined church with a burglar alarm
filibustering
      High and dry in the steeple.

Here then the young man came who wanted to eat and drink,
      To play, pray, make love;
Electronic voices nagged at him out of the filtered air,
      The eyes on the hoarding winked;
He knocked at the door of the house, the bears buzzed and
the flies
      Howled to him to come in.

Inside he found a table laid for two, a mirror
      Flanking the double bed,
On the night table a scent spray, a tin of biscuits, a bible,
      A crucifix on the wall
And beside it a comic postcard: all this he carefully noticed
      And then he noticed the floor

Bomb-pocked with tiny holes, from one of which there rose
        One tiny wisp of white.
He watched as it clawed the air two inches from the floor
        And saw it for what it was,
The arm of a girl, he watched and just could hear her voice
        Say: Wait! Wait till I grow.

And the arm grew and he wished to bend and clutch the hand
        But found he could no more move,
The arm grew and the fingers groped for help, the voice
        That had grown with the arm, the voice
That was now a woman's about to be saved or lost was calling
        For help. He could not move.

Then everything buzzed and boomed. The chaps outside on
  the lamp posts
        Hooted, broke wind, and wept,
Men the size of flies dropped down his neck while the
  mansized
        Flies gave just three cheers
And he could not move. The darkness under the floor gave
  just
        One shriek. The arm was gone.

Good Dream

He woke in his usual room, decided
Feeling completely awake to switch
The reading lamp on and read—but where
Is the switch? No switch no light. No light
No chapter nor verse. Completely awake
He gropes for the switch and finds the book
He left in the dark but what is a book
Left in the dark? He feels the book
Suddenly gently taken away
By someone's hand and a warm voice
Begins, beginneth, aloud in the dark:
Here beginneth the first chapter—
But it wasn't the first, he was half way through.
No, says the voice, *the first chapter
At the first verse in the first voice,
Which is mine, none other's: Here beginneth—*
But I tell you, he says, I was half way through,
I am completely awake, I can prove it;
Where is the switch? I will show you the place
Half way through.
                    There is no switch,
The voice replies; *in the beginning
Is darkness upon the face of the earth
In which you must wait for me till I
Show you the place not half way through
But just begun, the place you never
Knew was here.*
                    But I know this place,
It is my usual room, except
The switch has gone.

The switch was never
There to start with; which is why
You refuse to wake.

But I am completely
Awake, I told you.

You will tell me
Once you are. Here beginneth—
I tell you this is my usual room;
I can put out my hand from the bed and feel the . . .
Yes?

The wall—but I can't. Where
Has the wall gone? My bed was against it.
What was against it?

Why is your voice
Moving away? Why do I hear
Water over it?

There is water
Between us, I am here on the bank,
You will have to row.

Row?

What
Is a boat for? I am here on the bank.
But I need light to row.

No.
No light until you reach this bank.
Feel for your oars.

Here are my oars.
Then loose that rope. Are you ready? Row.
Here beginneth. . . .

He dips his oars
And knows the walls receding, hears
The ripples round the chair legs, hears
Larksong high in the chimney, hears

Rustling leaves in the wardrobe, smells
All the smells of a river, and yet
Feeling, smelling, hearing, knowing,
Still cannot see. This boat has no
Switch. No switch no light.
                              No light?
Pull on your oars. I am here.
                              He pulls.
Splutter of water, crackle and grinding
Of reeds and twigs; then bump. The hand
That stole the book that was left in the dark
Comes out of the dark, the hand that is hers,
Hers, none other's, and seizes his
To help him on to the bank.
                              'And God
Said Let there be light'.
                              His usual room
Has lost its usual walls and found
Four walls of sky, incredible blue
Enclosing incredible green enclosing
Her, none other.
                  Completely awake.

Selva Oscura

A house can be haunted by those who were never there
If there was where they were missed. Returning to such
Is it worse if you miss the same or another or none?
The haunting anyway is too much.
You have to leave the house to clear the air.

A life can be haunted by what it never was
If that were merely glimpsed. Lost in the maze
That means yourself and never out of the wood
These days, though lost, will be all your days;
Life, if you leave it, must be left for good.

And yet for good can be also where I am,
Stumbling among dark treetrunks, should I meet
One sudden shaft of light from the hidden sky
Or, finding bluebells bathe my feet,
Know that the world, though more, is also I.

Perhaps suddenly too I strike a clearing and see
Some unknown house—or was it mine?—but now
It welcomes whom I miss in welcoming me;
The door swings open and a hand
Beckons to all the life my days allow.

All Over Again

As if I had known you for years drink to me only if
Those frontiers had never changed on the mad map of the
  years
And all our tears were earned and this were the first cliff
From which we embraced the sea and these were the first
  words
We spread to lure the birds that nested in our day
As if it were always morning their dawnsong theirs and ours
And waking no one else me and you only now
Under the brow of a blue and imperturbable hill
Where still time stands and plays his bland and hemlock pipe
And the ripe moment tugs yet declines to fall and all
The years we had not met forget themselves in this
One kiss ingathered world and outward rippling bell
To the rim of the cup of the sky and leave it only there
Near into far blue into blue all over again
Notwithstanding unique all over all again
Of which to speak requires new fires of the tongue some trick
Of the light in the dark of the muted voice of the turning
  wild
World yet calm in her storm gay in her ancient rocks
To preserve today one kiss in this skybound timeless cup
Nor now shall I ask for anything more of future or past
This being last and first sound sight on eyes and ears
And each long then and there suspended on this cliff
Shining and slicing edge that reflects the sun as if
This one Between were All and we in love for years.